Lost Partners

Judith Saunders

FUTURECYCLE PRESS

www.futurecycle.org

Published by FutureCycle Press
Lexington, Kentucky, USA

ISBN 978-1-938853-80-7

For Nan

celebrating an astonishing oeuvre in
paint, clay, and mixed media

Contents

Artist...7

Double Portrait...9

Photocollages...10

Deux Femmes Pottery Bowl..12

Pottery Dessert Plates with Cat Portraits...........................13

Tile Tray: Mosaic Moose...14

House of Air...16

House of Water...18

Snow Image...20

Seashore Cartoon...22

Jack-in-the-Pulpit...23

Goddesses..24

Buddha and Cave..25

Alternative Crèche..26

Head Study...28

Alaskan Treasure Chest...30

Watercolor Sunset, Wappinger Creek..................................32

Mixed-Media Mobile...33

Artist and Audience..34

Elder Brother with Alzheimer's...35

Lost Partners..36

Acknowledgments

Artist

Elaborate drawings filled your notebooks,
crowded the margins of memoranda:
caricatures of boring speakers,

portraits of colleagues, anatomically
intricate close-ups of flowers
and insects, fantastical landscapes

harboring genial monsters. Formal
efforts with oil, ink, watercolor
or charcoal you sometimes (not often)

finished and framed. When you worked with clay
you left the studio with hand-shaped
pottery designs, one-of-kind

and minimally useful—no sets
of dinnerware for twelve. Did we need
a lidded pot shaped exactly like a bulb

of garlic? A serving dish for olives—
long and narrow, slightly crooked—stamped
with symbols from the Chinese zodiac?

No medium contented or contained
your exuberant invention: it spilled
from one enticing process to the next.

You felted wool, pressed flowers and weeds,
tried your hand at decoupage, mosaic,
photography, collage, assemblages,

integrating natural objects, artful
fragments and discarded junk—
a connoisseur of found materials.

You squeezed polymer through yard-sale
pasta makers, happily unwinding
strands of clay spaghetti. There was nothing

you wouldn't sink in grout. Our home was crammed
with your supplies: glue and sponges, brushes,
pencils, paints and pens, cardboard and twine,

glitter and shellac. You bought tools
for cutting, gripping, piercing, punching,
for stamping designs on paper and clay.

Crossing boundaries of style and genre,
unquenchably experimental,
you sizzled with new ideas, racing

through craft stores and collectible stalls
in quest of oddments corresponding
to your vision. Offbeat materials,

especially, inspired you—misshapen
gourds, an old doll's head. Often at night
you lay awake, the crafting spirit

strong in you, pondering a project:
that hollowed emu egg, the seaweed fronds
and iridescent abalone chips

you planned to fasten to its blue-green shell,
transporting the bird that might have been
to ocean depths it never would have known.

Double Portrait

[paper and paint]

Paper spread with gouache, folded
and scrunched: decalcomania
(even the name sounds dangerous)

provides the background that is also
foreground in this picture of a maelstrom.
Shades of foaming blues and whites

swirl toward an azure axis,
the eye of a blossom with tattered,
windmilling petals. In the middle

of that deep-blue vortex you've pasted
our images, cut from a photograph.
Side by side, wearing swimsuits, we smile

and wave, two tiny figures submerged
past the hips, surrounded by churning winds
and waters, bathed in unearthly light.

Irresistible forces—thrilling,
threatening—are sweeping us
away. We continue to smile,

our arms around each other's waists.
Wherever we are headed,
we are going there together.

Photocollages

Arranging in collages
snapshots of the two of us,
you scissored window shapes,
pieced together crazy quilts
of vivid instants—
fixed them fast—framed us

swishing slowly back and forth
on the great blue wooden swing
in the garden of our P-Town
B&B, reclining, languid
on the canopied bed, posing
for mid-life glamour portraits...

serving Chocolate Cabbage Cake
we baked together, all-day
project, for your fifty-first,
each cruciferous leaf
deliciously replicated
in confectioner's cacao...

waving holiday hellos
from a gleaming, true-red sleigh
hitched to actual reindeer...
peering, intrigued, at thermal pools
of roiling sludge, near Rotorua,
through veils of sulphurous steam...

dancing at home, miming
lyrics to Lacy J. Dalton's
"Wild Turkey," a stomping
strut in two-four time
around the living room,
fists on hips and elbows flapping...

riding a camel, mounted
double, you behind me,
the beast rising to its feet
rear end first, tilting you skyward
as you raise one arm, triumphant,
defying gravity....

Deliberately you gathered
and preserved the heres and nows,
juxtaposing one amusing, one
amazing moment with another,
illustrating as we lived it
our unlikely, lucky love.

Deux Femmes Pottery Bowl

In the bottom of this clay bowl
you copied our favorite Picasso
in relief, *Deux Femmes Calligraphiées,*

simplified but recognizable.
A bold, continuous line
draws two women together,

scribbles locks of wavy hair
curlicuing into gowns,
dabs facetious hints

of breast and belly, scrawls
lightly touching shoulders,
casually folded arms,

pairs an ordinary two
inseparably
with calligraphic flourish. You,

inspired imitator, chose to work
with brick-red clay, malleable
medium, tracing fluid contours

in three dimensions. Scooping
and smoothing, your fingers molded
palpable connectedness.

Pottery Dessert Plates with Cat Portraits

[pottery and paint]

Tuxedo cat, half Siamese,
her face heraldic with chevrons,
three inverted v's, sharply
symmetrical—black-white-black—
corralling the impudent scowl.

Tortoiseshell, half Persian,
perpetually owl-eyed
(all demure astonishment),
her coat a satin field
of dark, autumnal disarray.

Tile Tray: Mosaic Moose

[pottery tiles, glass, enamel]

To make this double line
of otherworldly moose

you molded, painted, fired
six tiles, each depicting

one proud profile:
palmate antlers, gleaming

turquoise eye, the pointed,
large-toed hoofs. Next step:

you broke each tile in half,
vertically, with one

decisive blow, boldly
fracturing the image

(so much for careful
artistry), sandwiching

between the front and rear
of each bisected moose

a slice of tile inscribed
with runic signs: swirls

and x's in bright teal
and amber. Floating,

saddle-like, these symbols
join the severed parts

of plain brown bodies,
lightly holding them

together, gathering
cryptic inner forces.

You laid out every beast
with care, forequarters

higher than the rumps,
stair-step physiology

creating the illusion
of a marching movement.

Opalescent moons (rounds
of glass) hover above

the mystic-marked procession,
light the way to risky

destinations, brave routes
to complex wholeness.

House of Air

[mixed media]

Exhilarated by heights, longing
to be airborne, you swayed
on narrow seats of mile-high
ski lifts, leaning into views,
the drop to sharp-toothed cliffs below.
Fearlessly you drove up steepest
grades, loosely graveled mountain roads,

skidding around the hair-pin turns,
gleefully skirting precipices.
You rode on monster roller coasters,
savoring moments when sheer force
(counter-gravitational)
would lift you from your seat,
propel you nearly into free fall.

This gabled wooden box, tall
and narrow, meant for housing
butterflies, you dedicated
to powers of air. Assorted birds
and insects, enameled metal
or polymer, have landed
on its sky-blue roof and walls.

You added nesting boxes filled
with wisps of straw and spotted eggs.
Among the starlings and dragonflies
you included unspectacular
aerial artists—grasshoppers,
beetles—whose brief and buzzing bursts
of levitation still amazed you.

To the housetop, unexpectedly,
you fixed a chime, a silver tube
balanced horizontally,
beside it a wooden striker,
inviting passersby to launch
its single note (a clear, high tone)
into airy weightlessness.

House of Water

[mixed media]

Summer your season, swimming
your sport, Pisces your sign,
you loved water for its buoyancy,
translucent touch resisting
and returning your embrace.

To celebrate that elemental bond
you made a house-shaped box,
rectangular, with sloping roof,
glass-paneled front and back.
Dried seaweed, stones and shells

encrust the outside edges.
To the roof and solid side walls
you glued handmade tiles, each
depicting a familiar waterscape:
Candlewood Lake (*the dock and raft,*

the family summer cottage,
baptismal diving and dunking),
Greenwich Point (*motherhood, beach walks,*
shovels, pails and sandcastles),
The Hudson (*viewed from your bedroom*

window in Dobbs Ferry, sailboats
and barges, the willow flowering
hugely on its bank—electrified
by lightning one heated summer night),
Herring Cove (*sand dunes and beach*

plum blossoms, half-mile swims,
bare-breasted bobbling in the surf),

Green Hills Pool (*neighbors, friends*
impressed for more than thirty years
with your tireless freestyle).

Inside the box, clearly visible
behind the glass, you piled
marbles, sparkling blues and greens,
simulating waves. A starfish
navigates the bumpy depths.

Floating above: a pale-green boat
loaded with golden sequins
(tiny coins) and a glass jug
labeled "Honey." A porcelain owl
and pussycat, fully provisioned,

peer alertly from the bow,
set to sail strange seas.
They crave tropical adventuring,
witty song and moonlit dance,
salt taste of eccentric romance.

Snow Image

She stretches out full length
on our canvas recliner,
a chalky figure absorbed
in her book. Posing

flat on her back, long legs,
upward-pointing toes, bent arms
obscuring smallish breasts
and slender waist, she makes

an unselfconscious nude.
She attests to your talents
as portraitist, moreover,
her resemblance to me

unmistakable. You piled
loose snow to sculpt her shape
(no icy chiseling), achieved
a softness in outline,

the naturalness of flesh.
Meltingly mortal, she looks as if
she might at any moment stir
to start her chair in rocking motion.

Her round blue sunshades lend
the only color to this grey-lit,
all-white scene, a field of snow
instead of sandy beach. Wintry

materials, summer theme:
a tour de force in whimsy,
happy contradiction.
Photography preserves the concept,

the brilliant neutrals: *Winter Nude,*
our most successful Christmas card,
your morning's work well squandered
in ephemeral creation.

Seashore Cartoon

[ballpoint pen, notebook paper]

To replace the carrying sack—
somehow gone missing—
for our purple beach umbrella,
you brought home a *gun case.*
Hauling our gear from car to beach
at Herring Cove, far end,

wearing khaki sun hats
with jutting brims and neck-flaps,
Foreign Legion fashion,
we looked like terrorists
on holiday. You sketched us
sternly marshaling cooler,

towels, canvas chairs,
umbrella (snug as a rifle
in its brand-new pouch)
—prepared, evidently,
to defend to the hilt
one quilt-sized swatch of sand.

Jack-in-the-Pulpit

[watercolor on paper]

In your watercolor study
of *Arisaema triphyllum,*

the flowering cowl bulges
in the foreground, rounded

and creamy, elegant bauble
striped vertically in brown

like Victorian patterns
for ladies' dress goods,

its hooded folds and ribboning
upthrust, small surprise, between

drenched greens of stalk and leaves,
swelling with festive promise.

Goddesses

[mixed media]

In this display case, surely meant
for mounting insects, you arranged
your collection of ancient totems,
deities, amulets, all unlabeled,

faceless female figures wielding
bows and arrows, lifting tridents,
baring glories of buttocks, breasts
and bellies, signing blessings,

dispensing balm, hoisting aloft
a moonstone sphere. Animals
accompany them (a bear, a cat, a deer),
familiars and companions.

Surrounding all these figures
you laid down quartz in nuggets,
quiet shades of amber, violet,
blue and green—deliberately

placed to frame and protect—
invoking natural magic
of circle and stone. Centered
at the bottom of the case

lies a watch face, abruptly
futuristic, a reminder
that no gods, no creeds, no dreams
of heaven have endured. Only

the gritty mysteries of flesh
and bone persist, the hungers
of the body, the earth itself
with its jewels and its curves.

Buddha and Cave

[clay, bronze]

A seated Buddha, two inches tall,
occupies your pottery cave, filling
its emptiness with his bronze presence.
The hollow space you've made,
a flat-floored, arching oval,
stands open on one side. Pocked
with indentations from your pressing

fingers, the outside surface is uneven.
Patchy glazing adds texture. Camouflage
colors—dull, dark green on khaki brown,
crudely mottled—complete the earthy
effect. This free-standing cavern,
extracted from a handy mountain,
looks ancient, overgrown with moss.

The shelter it offers is incomplete:
the top of its sloping roof is pierced
with holes, pencil-sized, in two neat rows.
(Why? Did you prop the roof with sticks
to keep it from collapsing in the kiln?)
Buddha sits—dignified, unmoving—
in his leaky hermitage.

He declines to set out buckets
or shift position—to dodge
the spear-like rivulets of rain
and fiercely gusting downdrafts.
Knowing all is transitory
(the weather sure to change),
he affirms a wise inertia.

Alternative Crèche

[clay, wood, paper, metal]

Crude but expressive, your clay figures
reenact the Nativity, modify
iconic tradition. Instead

of sitting stiffly upright to display
an infant posing, regal, on her lap,
Mary relaxes in the straw, comfortably

reclining, first-time mother
exhausted from childbirth. She holds
her baby close to her breast.

She smiles: to her, at this moment,
he is the most important being
in the world. Two large beasts

of uncertain species, neither sheep
nor camel—cattle perhaps?—
settle, recumbent, by the manger.

Close inspection reveals holes, punched
in clay behind the ears, anchor-points
for horns or antlers—and, yes,

here in the box are four small twigs,
nicely branching, to insert.
Heads tilted attentively,

two oddly bovine antelope
bear calm witness to new life.
Three blue-robed female figures

approach in friendly fashion,
offering gifts. One brings a broom,
another bread (how realistically

you shaped and scored that loaf).
A third woman carries stacks
of cleaning cloths. They have spread

a basket of fruit, a bunch of roses,
a bottle of wine invitingly
before the tired Madonna.

Off to the side, Joseph sits huddled
at a fire made from sparkling paper
flaring up in a nest of wire. He stares

down into sharp-edged flames,
rubbing his hands, countenance
bewildered. Meanwhile

the visitors arrange their gifts,
practical things for immediate use,
small luxuries to comfort and to cheer:

flowers, fruit, and wine. Mother and child
rest peacefully, everything
miraculously ordinary.

Head Study

[mixed media]

On styrofoam balls—one black,
one silver—you fastened
matching plastic masks,
inserting behind the eyeholes
flattened ovals, dichroic glass,
to gaze opaquely outward.

Headbands—a braided rope
with geometric figures (Navaho
gone Hippie), a pastel ribbon
of two-toned sequins—wrap
around the makeshift foreheads,
defining brows. Earrings, abalone

set in silver, frame each gleaming
countenance, complementing
lustrous complexions. Top
and back, in place of hair,
ornaments erupt in willful
assemblage: copper wheels,

titanium horseshoes,
origami cranes, glass beads,
a miniature crystal-studded
wand (relic of Harmonic
Convergence). Paper petals,
hardy and insistent,

burst in bunches
from glistening scalps.
Small, embellished boxes

with removable lids, firmly
implanted in skull-bone,
open two-way traffic

with galactic interiors,
channel irrepressible
intent...this metal tin, labeled
WAY OUT, a souvenir
from London's Underground,
hatchway to a starry elsewhere.

Alaskan Treasure Chest

[mixed media]

Filled with tourist treasure, jumbled
park brochures and maps, wildlife
guidebooks, photographs and postcards,
ticket stubs from ferries, trains, museums,
this miniature wooden pirate's chest
cannot contain Alaska—big
boisterous 49th state.

Denali has poked its icy peak
through the lid, straining skyward
in full color. Fantastical salmon,
Juno's answer to Chicago's *Cow Parade,*
have swum through cracks in the sides,
somersaulting nonchalantly
across one blue-stained panel.

Native carvings and figurines—
Yup'ik, Inupiac, Haida—
have staked their claim front and back.
A feather-trimmed, ancient face of horn
shapes its mouth in astonishment.
A mermaid of the North—half woman,
half seal—drifts by on walrus bone.

A staring, soapstone crone displays
her ever-fertile, bright-green bosom.
On a slab of darkened antler,
patiently etched, a massive bear
observes two spouting whales
while line on line on line conjures
silence: ocean, cloud, black sun.

Through the one remaining panel
of the still-unopened chest, a stream
has forced its way; someone is panning
there for gold. Sled dogs, too,
have escaped from the interior,
a circle of friendly muzzles and fur
with you at its smiling center.

Watercolor Sunset, Wappinger Creek

Watery smudges of backlit cloud
trickle down the canvas to meet
their own reflection: sky and water
blur in dusky pinks and golds.

In the corner, lower right,
a dark form strains skyward,
Blue Heron lifting itself
from the creek, right wing extended

to beat the air, its diagonal thrust
targeting the topmost center
of the scene where a sun (orange
circle with yellow nimbus) pauses

at the tree line, puddling the water
with a few last drips of light.
Clumps of reeds, sparsely distributed,
darken in the foreground of fading day.

You did not paint the highway
at your back, just outside the frame,
all monotonous pavement
and impatient engines, devoid

of elemental peace and purpose.
You could have named your composition
almost unironically
Commute Hour at Wappinger Creek:

day on its rose-splotched journey
into night...clouds calmly streaming
in unrehearsed directions...
Blue Heron bound for Bali H'ai.

Mixed-Media Mobile

[clay, root, fabric]

Inspired by a tree root—twisted
and knobbed, with two long
trailing laterals—you shaped
and painted a head from clay,
a face softly smiling, homely
and humanoid. You clamped it,

fired and finished, to the front end
of the root—with dismaying results:
an armless torso dragging a pair
of spindly, useless legs. Struck
by second thoughts (*maybe this
is backwards*), you stuck the head

on the other end of the root,
inverting your design. In a flash
those limbs became arms, long
and graceful, powerful as wings,
stretching up and outward
past the sideways-tilted head:

your creature was alive
and flying. You added a shirt,
attached a string, and set him
swinging in our kitchen. There
he soars, released from earth
to air, to unimagined bliss.

Artist and Audience

The unexpected was your signature,
tucked away in some far corner

of the piece, behind a door, beneath
a lid, something to explore, to touch,

perhaps to set in motion,
interactive—a knob to twirl,

a cap to twist, a latch to lift,
each an invitation:

Open the box. Admire the scarab,
shark's tooth, minute millefiori frog

secreted there. Pass your fingers over
hard-edged ridges, cool smoothness.

Unroll the onionskin papyrus
to encounter lines by Wallace Stevens,

Emily Dickinson, copied out
in Lilliputian script. Feel free

to use the bright containers
set in grout or glued to wood

(unlikely, integral components
of mixed-media assemblage)

to store things of your own:
a special ring or souvenir,

a bottle cap, a key: Improvise
additions to a boisterous medley.

Elder Brother with Alzheimer's

[mixed media]

To make this sad and horrible piece
you scavenged a soccer ball, gray
and limp, smeared on textured paste,
and wound it round with tangles
of yarn, neurofibrillary fuzz,
twisted fibers strangling thought.

That gruesomely festooned,
deflated brain you mounted
on the base of a dismantled
music box, plastering wood panels
with photographs, a lifetime
of irreclaimable selves:

youthful soldier escorting home
his glamorous bride, Church Deacon
mustering a congregation,
engineer designing skis and poles
for handicapped young athletes,
amateur historian posed

with ice-cutting tool collection,
Man-of-the-Mountain leading
a llama up Mt. Washington,
patriarch feasting at family clambake
(three generations of descendants),
retiree trekking in Katmandu.

The music box still plays. From time
to time you cranked the handle,
watched the photos and flaccid head
revolving slowly to a tune, "The Way We
Were": interactive art, grotesque
as the unmaking of a brother's mind.

Lost Partners

[mixed media]

Embedded, one by one, in grout,
these earrings without mates
fill but do not crowd the showcase,
a bewildering array
of sizes, shapes, materials:
witty creations in plastic
or paper, solid pieces made

from glass or hammered metals,
some set with semiprecious stones.
Relics of craft fairs and boutiques,
they point to bygone anniversaries
and Christmases, birthday trips
and celebrations. They stand
for what is missing, what is lost.

To frame these salvaged remnants
you devised a border of glass,
interspersing squares of teal green
with rounds of purple. Empty space
throughout you filled with chips
of pastel quartz. Up close
it's all just planless scatter

(like the randomness of loss)
but with distance a design
appears, subtly converging
toward a silver center:
not an earring but a pendant.
The simple disk, lightly etched
to depict a quail (your favorite bird),

was handmade by your favorite brother,
now dead, in the metal-working years
of his retirement, to seal a bond
predating others. Just above
the pendant you placed a watch,
the double doors of its case
pried open to expose an old

unmoving face. It is in time
that things—and the people
who bestow and cherish them
(cherish *us*)—go missing. All
we can do is what you have done
here, rearranging what is left,
piece by piece, to honor what is gone.

Acknowledgments

Individual poems have appeared in periodicals, as follows:

The Gay and Lesbian Review: "Watercolor Sunset, Wappinger Creek"
South Carolina Review: "Artist"

Cover artwork, Ewen Kua's photo of Lost Partners *by Nancy K. McCormick; cover and interior book design by Diane Kistner; Charter text with Advent Pro titling*

About FutureCycle Press

FutureCycle Press is dedicated to publishing lasting English-language poetry books, chapbooks, and anthologies in both print-on-demand and ebook formats. Founded in 2007 by long-time independent editor/publishers and partners Diane Kistner and Robert S. King, the press incorporated as a nonprofit in 2012. A number of our editors are distinguished poets and writers in their own right, and we have been actively involved in the small press movement going back to the early seventies.

The FutureCycle Poetry Book Prize and honorarium is awarded annually for the best full-length volume of poetry we publish in a calendar year. Introduced in 2013, our Good Works projects are anthologies devoted to issues of universal significance, with all proceeds donated to a related worthy cause. Our Selected Poems series highlights contemporary poets with a substantial body of work to their credit; with this series we strive to resurrect work that has had limited distribution and is now out of print.

We are dedicated to giving all of the authors we publish the care their work deserves, making our catalog of titles the most diverse and distinguished it can be, and paying forward any earnings to fund more great books.

We've learned a few things about independent publishing over the years. We've also evolved a unique, resilient publishing model that allows us to focus mainly on vetting and preserving for posterity the most books of exceptional quality without becoming overwhelmed with bookkeeping and mailing, fundraising activities, or taxing editorial and production "bubbles." To find out more about what we are doing, come see us at www.futurecycle.org.

www.ingramcontent.com/pod-product-compliance
Lightning Source LLC
Chambersburg PA
CBHW060044050426
42448CB00012B/3119